you are everything you are not

Also by John High

Ceremonies
Sometimes Survival
the lives of thomas: episodes and prayers
all along her thighs
(selected writings translated into Russian by Nina Iskrenko)
The Sasha Poems
The Desire Notebooks
Bloodline: Selected Writings
here
a book of unknowing

as translator
Blue Vitriol by Aleksei Parshchikov
(with Michael Molner and Michael Palmer)
The Right to Err: Selected Poems of Nina Iskrenko
(with Patrick Henry and Katya Olmsted)
The Inconvertible Sky by Ivan Zhdanov (with Patrick Henry)

as editor
Crossing Centuries: The New Generation in Russian Poetry
(ed. with Vitaly Chernetsky, Thomas Epstein, Edward Foster,
Lyn Hejinian, Patrick Henry, Gerald Janecek, Vadim Mesyats,
Leonard Schwartz, and Laura Weeks)

john high

you are everything you are not

(the third book in a trilogy
following *here* and
a book of unknowing)

talisman house, publishers
2013 • greenfield, massachusetts

Published in the United States of America by
Talisman House, Publishers
P.O. Box 896
Greenfield, Massachusetts 01302

Manufactured in the United States of America

12 13 14 7 6 5 4 3 2 1 FIRST EDITION

ISBN: 978-1-58498-095-7

Text: Palatino

Book designed by Samuel Retsov

For Andrea

Even the deaf-mute has an expression. Do not judge that she cannot possess any expression. Those who create expressions are not necessarily limited to the ones who are not deaf-mute, for the deaf mute does express. His voice should be heard and his utterance should be heeded. Unless you identify yourself with her, how can you meet him? How can you talk with her?

—Dogen

This entire mistake once activated is thus come, even looking someplace else, there is no place else. There is only the expression of the deaf-mute and the silence of speaking and hearing.

—Kotatsu Roko

Everything, all that I understand, I understand, only because I love.

—Leo Tolstoy

Contents

the ghostwoman, the monk, & a girl
on a red scooter with a transistor radio

floating on the raft of a book

Preface

In preparation for writing this preface, I decided to reread some of John High's previous books. The reason for rereading, aside from the sheer pleasure of re-encountering High's work, is that *you are everything you are not*, as the third book in his trilogy, is quite naturally a continuation of the concerns he expressed in both *here* and, even more in *a book of unknowing*. I must confess that my numerous bookshelves are not terribly well organized. Which is to say: I had to do a search. I found *a book of unknowing* without much difficulty. It took me a while, however, to locate *here*. Finally, it made its presence known. It was sandwiched between Bunyan's *The Pilgrim's Progress* and Dōgen's *Moon in a Dewdrop*. I chuckled, at first, at the odd juxtaposition, likening it to Lautréamont's "fortuitous meeting on a dissecting table of a sewing-machine and an umbrella." But the more I thought about it, I came to feel that this peculiar grouping of texts was not at all surreal; it was more the music of chance, where chance acts as a true guide that obliquely points the way forward or inward. It was an opening not so unlike that described by High in "Dialogue XXI:"

...a sky so keen in arrival that observation
in a letter opens to the meeting of apples
on the table between them—all the moments
to come and redemptive stones in a glass
cup where the girl holds the tip of a rose
& these parables we call forth in an imagined
passage of days & boats on water.

Let me explain. Bunyan's tale is an allegorical account of a pilgrim's journey over terrain packed with pitfalls. Dōgen addresses, among many things, how best to navigate and decipher the Way. *you are everything you are not* attempts to turn the Way into a tangible experience of acting, listening, and feeling. In High's poems, a mute girl and a one-eyed boy traverse a torturous and tortured landscape, both natural and manufactured, a landscape of lost and found, of shape shifters and ghosts and a prominent ghostwoman, of monks and hermit nuns and fish and birds who mouth words that the mute girl cannot. Neither Sloughs of Despond nor Delectable Mountains are specifically named, though there are swamps and mountains. But compared to these two wanderers, Bunyan's Christian had it much easier. He had the Celestial City as an end point for his perilous journey. The mute girl and the one-eyed boy are not journeying toward something. They are simply in motion, beings among beings, beings unto themselves. Salvation does not await; in the finding is the seeking, in the seeking the finding.

you are everything you are not, like all of High's work, is a dazzling complexity of sight, sound and breath as the poet grapples with the Way. Lyrical, tense and haunting, these poems evoke the internal and external struggles to remain engaged with and in each moment, to see that the truth is not outside ourselves but within us. As the mute girl and the one-eyed boy venture across the obstacle-laden earth, their tasks, like that of the poet, are to cast aside illusion and delusion; even conscious enlightenment must be tossed away until it is so integrated into being that it becomes traceless.

The girl remembered
how, remembered the remembering
of that which cannot be touched
and only seen in an unseeing, here, in
an inanimate trace of our nearness...

In *The Genjōkōan* Dōgen writes: "To study the Way is to study the self. To study the self is to forget the self. To forget the self is to be enlightened by all things of the universe. To be enlightened by all things of the universe is to cast off the body and mind of the self as well as those of others. Even the traces of enlightenment are wiped out, and life with traceless enlightenment goes on forever and ever."

What we have in *you are everything you are not* is a literary and imaginary response to Dōgen's words. Like all texts that truly matter, the book can and should be read on many levels. There is first the compelling story of these two wanderers. High acutely focuses on incident and action, on their worldly and other-worldly encounters, on their consistent courage, on compassion as a form of love and love as a form of compassion. He reveals them as wise learners, even (and perhaps most especially) in their often frustrated but always heroic attempts to comprehend what is happening around them. The universe in which his characters ramble is a realm as magically realistic as any found in a García Márquez novel, but in High there is an added dimension, namely that of the "sheer human beauty and terror of consciousness." This, for High and his characters, is the pronounced principle of existence itself.

Interpenetrating the worldly events is a decided concern with knowing and remembering and willfulness at keeping on: "If you have come this far, why stop now?" Contained within each dialogue is a meditation on what is the Way, on what is the self, on what is the role we are best suited to play in this flesh-and-blood world where "figures of syllables & parable / pause between words." In this sense, High is illuminating what practice is. To practice the Way is, in itself, enlightenment, yet High is careful not to insist that enlightenment is somehow superior to simply being. They are one and the same. The mute girl and the one-eyed boy are not portrayed as conscious seekers of enlightenment. And yet enlightenment, in its myriad forms, possibilities and prospects, is also consistently theirs.

High constructs his discourse through the ancient teaching form in both the east and the west of dialogue. And while the interlocutors change from dialogue to dialogue, and even within the dialogue, the focus is very much on asking questions. As in a koan, answers are less pronounced, less direct, and while occasionally skewed, or seemingly so, are never tangential to the particular problem being posed. It is a masterful device, for it keeps the narrative continually evolving while also mirroring the practice of the Way.

Language, of course, is the medium of transmittal but High is also acutely aware of the paltriness of words to convey inner experience. Indeed, language, as every Zen practitioner comes to know quite quickly and intimately, is at times an obstacle to saying what needs to be said:

…To speak of love,
an untamed signature of words holds
no yesterday or tomorrow, the ghostwoman
says, pages falling in around
as she steps forward…

High also realizes that language is limiting, that in some ways it is a paradox to use words to explain what is inaccessible to and for language. In many ways this is the theme of "Dialogue VII" in which the koan-like conversation focuses on what can and can't be said:

Language is a place.
Perhaps you are mistaken.

Our mother was sleeping, not aware when death came.
The storyteller has no other home.

And:

The story never leaves you.
What is your calling?
You think I am a tale, but this is simply a face you've forgotten.
In another vocabulary we were talking in a theatre.
Yet you were only a dream.
And the language you call home—human figures moving across
    white meadows covered by black cormorants.
Is that why you have come?

And yet language, despite its limitations, is the only medium to construct experience. Even the mute girl speaks, since the only way to convey her thoughts and understanding and questioning is through words.

The concerns in *you are everything you are not* began to surface in *The Desire Notebooks* of 1999. And though the one-eyed boy and other figures make their first appearances in that volume, the philosophical reflections become more apparent and realized in the two books preceding this one: *here* and *a book of unknowing*. Indeed, *you are everything you are not* is by far the most thorough working out of these ideas. This is not to say that this is (nor should be) the last book in this cycle, which like the best Zen commentaries, is a tremendous mix of conundrums and reflections, and above all, questions. Nor should this long discursive meditative journey be seen as some sort of linear delineation. High's progression, like *zazen*, itself, is not step-by-step. It is vast and varied, where each arrival is also a new starting point: "so you discovered the beginning & / inquire about the end?"

—Christopher Sawyer-Lauçanno
Turners Falls, Massachusetts
18 February 2013

saying that
the unsaid said
seeing sorrow,
surrender, serenity,
sovereignty.

> —a mute girl in Hangzhou
> *Dragon Diaries*
> 546 A.D.

A one-eyed boy turns to my circus man who has led him to the city. "I have eyes, ears, nose, tongue and no eyes, ears, nose, tongue—and no mind," the boy says when he finds the girl again at the master's grave.

> —a one-eyed boy at Mevlānā's grave
> *The Circus Man's Journals*
> Konya, Anatolia, 1273

The ghostwoman trailing over a ridge behind them—

The moon shining over each.
A mute girl speaking.
No trace.
These leaves falling
on a ground of blood & snow.

you are everything you are not

(dialogues and interludes)

Prologue

The book of the unwritten, where did you find it?
The pages fallen in stones by river.
The unsaid saying a site of body & undressed wounds of the unborn?
My mouth will not at all be capable.
We found your waters, ghosted letters, a visible world yet unseen,
 voices come home to their own stories.
A nominative?
The gerundive, *the what should be*—the poet wrote before you. From
 where the beginning is, there should be your end.
A mute girl carrying a book?
She & the one-eyed boy traded it between their ears & eyes.
It was like looking out over talons on snow?
Words written on a mouth. When you take off your shame, no one
 will hide it under a bush.
All of your life we had waited.
Elegiac & bardic forms already in our wound, yes.
Still here, to hear, before an ear, an unending silence.
What were the stones of a river saying?
You enter once. And over and again.
All the same, the stone a stone—the vow a vow—and to meet in this
 auspicious way.

Is this what the stones were saying that night he left the city to again
 find her?

Taking no thought from morning until evening, and from evening until morning....The unwritten in a book without names—a one-eyed boy whispering in a mute girl's unspoken mouth, our circus man dancing by the side of a road, juggling burnt leaves, then taking hold of the handles of his bicycle.

Dialogue I
>a source of their wandering

Why are you born?

I came to learn the source of their wandering.

Who is in the place where you are going?

Why don't you ask me my name?

A sky & four horses & vast mountainside tonight.

On the other side of nothingness, what is our vanishing?

(The girl in red sneakers whistles down an alley.)

In the Book of Events I traced the source of their wandering.

If there are cliffs in our distances, who is their God?

Walking into words there is only an echo.

But what about the mute girl & boy: these geese & owls & turtles
    mingling by the hammock & swing?

The calm rain in sleep, yes.

Her skirt torn & bared arms and there are deserts behind waters and
    the clouds fly off.

I wanted to learn of their wandering, so you speak of things &
    inanimate restless beings?

The inanimate speaks.

If a name, you'd be trapped by it—is this a prison or prism of their
    language?

I hear passing terns & layers of white waves.

Entering where the gap between thoughts appear?

A monastic field within an eye where all roads disappear.

Nostalgia, the wind says backwards.

When the sky is still, yes—there is a return to stillness.

Dialogue II
    a girl of familiar kiss

...while being lived we came to you early one morning by cliffs & sea
    & later in canyons & cemeteries where we were happy to lose our
    shame.
        All those seams a certain size & color, how a one-eyed boy
            was coupled in flower & blood.
We saw a face & a tale itself telling itself of no abode.

A mute girl gesturing?
        Without sound. Fertile mouth. And a father in every least
            thing the unheard here seen.
It was her father?

Rather, a small boat in an eddy.
        Bees & deer where crows once flew to the eaves of a barn.

Forsaken?
        The nothing that is not no longer separate here, the crow
            squawks.

Low hanging skies, wow, a girl of familiar lip to eye, who breathes
    this air.
        No longer or other or of imagined things.

You see her sitting there by a transistor radio, a red scooter, lingering
    by a cypress grove in a black & orange t-shirt.
        A pear tree in winter sun, yes.

Or blackberries on a table tonight.
    All without and within a body listening.

Terns & gulls finding their way home, it is true.
    Not a thing or a sentence but what we have become?

Story & breath, two figures pausing to read comics by sea—the
    ghostwoman waves her
        hands in a winter howl.

If not in this, who?
        Yes, where else, if not here
        who else (where now) if not here.

Dialogue III
> the mute girls asks

What is it that is already here?

Animate stone, serene sorrow. Turning toward tracks & ridge where
the alphabet had fallen.

I am not afraid of your death, the ghostwoman caws, picking words
from her mouth.

A fisherman traipsing to this ravaged station after a thousand years?

I saw you in a drawing, the girl nods, leaning into horses.

Clouded in evening. The boy plays cards under a flight of wings.

When you were dead, these were fragments of bird & word left from
sky, the boy tells her.

That was when I was sleeping, the girl mouths back in a hovering.

As for myself, the silence of language has been most cherished.

> Boats gone ashore?

The one-eyed boy not written here, but he is at home in our
forgiveness, she stutters.

This is what is already here?

We are everything we are not.

Dialogue IV
  at the end of a word

It was in a final hour under elm & honeysuckle.
You had been in this place before?
Something that brought the girl & ghostwoman again. Sagebrush &
  pebble scattered among the stream of hair.
Personal longing, their days in the earth beginning? our circus man
  asks, rubbing his one good hand over her scabby palms.
Tattered sky, sun, the docks, a boy's beauty in a rot of beauty.
A fisherman helping and seals all about the sea.
The girl hears fish breathing and guesses it's the hour.
The boy in his black corduroy pants by docks in the bardo?
After we were finished translating their language, yes.
Between deaths?
Reading from the Book of Events.
I have never seen the book.
Stars plunging over horizon. Moments moored in masquerading.
  Pages & pipers all up & down shore.
You thought this was a secret?
Mixing up the Table of Contents wherever he walked, she washed his
  feet in salt water.
Their first kiss?
Pieces of a prayer on matchsticks.
By now she'd learned of his love?
Cormorant, sandpipers, shredded alphabets, signs, what else could
  we call it?
If it were theory she would not have come, you are right.
Darker birds & cartoons.

A mute girl sleeping in a broken down Oldsmobile.

Yet you who are you in the telling or do you still face the fate of a
    storyteller?

Small shells & husks of shells, only this we can attest to.

These are human figures gathering.

Before you even heard them in a wave?

As if it were the last thing.

The first thing she uttered to the boy.

The sound of her muteness.

Spitting out our wound.

The girl wandering outside time & language or straying inside the burn inside the boy's striped shirt, all these geese on ground & the lake of forgetting where the poet came & asked them for our identity cards. A commentary on the being dark & safe & receiving whom we know on that night. On that night her vocabulary growing inside & furtively so that no one saw beyond dawn—& the sweet house where they slept without disguise or need of explanation.

Dialogue V
> language shifting in a mouth

...the boy asks as they walk into our words.

These shadowed skyscrapers over-reaching an oyster bay.

As we stand back in sounds that are no longer, and never were, our
> own.

If we have all lived & died, why endless return in stillness?

A mute girl looks over the walls of a city.

The dusk of evening dust & a child with shaved head runs down a
> highway.

Looking eye to eye into the face of God?

The girl puts her sandal in the one-eyed boy's hand & tiptoes to
shore,
> imagining he is a boat.

But where does the prayer come from?

The boy grinning when he takes off her shoe.

A distant being of rain at sea?

Language shifting in her mouth.

Yet so many things untold of earth & water.

The unconditional image of only love, yes.

Leaves away & away into these cypress trees webbing away a road,
> and away in branches
and yes, away.

Why do you see only our blame? the girl asks the dead one whose
> eyes will not be unbroken.

A strand of hair left in wet weed earlier as the boy touched her ear.

The girl calls back with the call to prayer and birds suddenly fly up.

A raven on branches overhanging a gate.

Sharp mountains in the shape of crooked lines on a ghostwoman's
    hand.
We are not and not only here.
This is what she mouthed in the boy's ear that night he first departed
    the city to find her.

Dialogue VI
>   the ghostwoman & a game of soccer

A day in the life of snow on river and her ghost waiting outside their
>   tent.
>>   Was it something to give your life for?
>>   The girl was still trying to get home.
Fine white flakes in a grove of madrone?
She had signs, yet no one remained in the village of saying whom you
>   are like.
>>   Blackbirds & pelicans flying in from the manzanitas to the
>>   east, but she and the boy were no longer searching.
It had taken nine months to arrive, but her ghostwoman no longer
>   guiding.
The hermit-nun who appeared in her diary?
Released us to our fields, yes.
Over the cliff the one-eyed boy was counting cards. The monks with
>   their shaved heads, dressed up for a game of soccer.
Where was her mother?
Dead.
Then you must watch for the world.
But what is the dying?
Go over there for suggestions, the hermit called to her that final
>   evening, go over there….

Dialogue VII
     the monk of a ghost entering winter

It was winter and we were looking at a sky.
But why did you come again?
An hour of ravage.
The soft fur of coat & a mouth tender. The trees to the south full of
    snow.
Wandering in a namelessness I once met the boy.
What was he like?
A face forlorn, or was that laughter I saw in his eye?
The monks already walking, but we sensed they would arrive with
    the deepening of winter.
He was looking for his father.
The father was a signature you gave him. Yet the unborn face was
    there before he was born.
Walking through the snowy fields of another country?
It was winter and we were studying a sky.
The father leaning on a telephone pole, when I saw him at a final
    station of the first train heading home.
The trains departing?
I saw you there.
The mute girl carrying a basketful of blueberries.
That was the second time she heard us with her own ears.
What was she trying to say?
Strawberries, strawberries....
I wonder where she found them?
Language is a place.
Perhaps you are mistaken.

Our mother was sleeping, not aware when death came.

The storyteller has no other home.

I saw smoke rising along river and sensed we would find you
    alongside them.

Fields burning and surrounded by scorned raccoons & soldiers.

It was the only way.

I wish we had seen you the night the soldiers came. Perhaps we could
    have helped.

You were studying a sky. Now you have taught us to study a sky.

You and the girl watching us at the station. You thought I was going
    to die.

The story never leaves you.

What is your calling?

You think I am a tale, but this is simply a face you've forgotten.

In another vocabulary we were talking in a theatre.

Yet you were only a dream.

And the language you call home—human figures moving across
    white meadows covered by black cormorants.

Is that why you have come?

The hills & cliffs beyond there.

Here. This is the coat that was your father's. Now it is yours.

So you will walk with me?

It is the only way we can go now.

Dialogue VIII
> the things around here announce their names

…the sky a grey shape of cranes?
> So that his eyes will not be broken.

Three dark-haired children, only figures, skipping through mud in
pretty dresses down stream by sparrows.

Tree-tops hovering above a village below a window.

A wind in the mountain behind a thatched hut only a moment ago,
> yes.

Once I heard there was a monastery in these hills.
> Perhaps we should go out & find it?
> The mute girl is waiting.

How memory is a place?

The sky grey shapes of cranes coming inward in wind or word or
> other from sea.
> Can you see them?
> The things around hear & pronounce their shapes.
> The one-eyed boy following with a monk who gave him back
> his name.
> His name or mouth?
> There is no longer the same moon, the same river, the same
> cloud, it is true.

Whereas in speech we have regrets or longing, voices not of our own?

Nearsighted magpie, pear blossom, pissed soil, swan & egret &
> fecund earth of earlier ordered things.

Only moments ago, yes.

Maybe here in wind & mountain and they are simply remembering
   us?
I have an idea followed by a question, if you are listening.
Your nearness is all.

My circus man falling into the quickness of leaves.

Good morning, whales & dragons,
the girl caws.

In the name of the Book of Events there were no furtherings or commentaries, only sky & ridge, the elephant in a field & a boy skinny-dipping by an awesome creek, the orphaned sky & a mute girl asking what is it in a saying of loaves & fishes & the speaking too of manuscripts & bowls of rice & her eyes following his movement in water, the sparse spruce & pine around. Why did you never ask me if I love you she asked again & as the beginning of observations fell into inquiry the boy came ashore to tell her & only now standing, his figure naked before her, did she hear him among these damaged & blooming pear trees.

Dialogue IX
     where his mother is buried

The boy aware that she could not hear him?
So he learned to speak less often and even then without a mouth.

Nothing else, all these years of
elm in a conference of animals talking by caves & you.

     Is that why we travel together?
     To look in the same direction, yes.

In times of frost she would often share
a dirty coat of a bed & the way
he might throw his hand over her mutedness.

     And why are the deer always
     drifting in bright dew?

She gestures & points
to a blue ridge & fluttered hills,
where his mother is buried.

     O.

     A long time when you alas eased among our unborn.

A conflict of nations gone,

nothing more than albatross fluting over water.

An owl over talus, a cliff over an owl.

> The ghostwoman who follows
> through nights outside our cities.

What is it we see,
the boy asks his own face tonight.

A possum in a creek, ta ta says the circus man
humming as we step back.

> A noun of blush has become
> the property of the sovereign?

I see your wound and I accept it—the boy tiptoes over
(& licks both of her ears).
And this beginning
into remembering such
a curious thing.

An acorn falling from a gull's beak onto shells,
the circus man leaving the circus.

Dialogue X
    a boy and a bottom well

...so the story goes on and leaves you?

A garden outside a window where we first discovered a library of
    unwritten letters.
        Not that these were things, or objects, only dialogues with a
        sky appearing & disappearing, even then.

That every verb is a fiction, but what, then, the story?
        Watching the homeless girl skip about under a pear tree, for
        instance.

Now you are speaking of the child who saw herself becoming?
        Black earth and hornet's nest,
        the one great question overcoming her gait.

You saw?
        Who she is, yes.

Still you believed in the story
        we also saw vanishing beside her.

Traces of lizard tracks in damp soil
        where we find a girl's diary in a boat.
To live in a dream is to die in forgetfulness?

If you want to find the meaning
        stop chasing after things.

I see no one or one thing.
        And still, no mouth in a sky & no rose vine on a branch
        without distinction.

The boy needed to say it?
        To hear it unsaid.

The sheer human beauty & terror of consciousness.

But can you say it?
        I forgive you, yes. For even this, we love you.

I was a child once, the girl hums.
Everywhere we are not appears as a dream.
But it is not a dream.

Dialogue XI
      mending nets offshore

…a remembering of water?
      Go inside a question and your life becomes a question.
The way the monk smells a one-eyed boy's coat?
A small wave in the middle of waves.
Kissed in the forgotten way, we depart a torn light.
A blue house among birch trees lining the shore.
I was there once.
An island where the boats harbored them before we began.

      An opening inside a body,
      the rafting of a book?
      We've come to the place where
      they once paused, yes.

The boy & monk tending the docks at dawn.

      Mending nets off shore & in this we who remain.

Each has to tell of their own life and death.
Still, quiet sky, still, waves—still remembers itself.
      —as if awakened from a dream
      and falling into my own arms,
      what took you so long?
Whoever is our wound & wound in blessing
among deaf trees

brings shadows, almost tree-like, to the place of beginning.
    It has to express itself, yes.

Our own vanishing?

    If you run from it, it is not a true story,
    the monk told the boy as they drank
    plum wine from wooden boats over
    a hundred years ago

Missing you—to one day, one hour, one breath.
Bon voyage, until we meet again & again & always.

Dialogue XII
      questions of birth

The girl on a spiral stair in a field near Dongshan's Temple:
      bundles of wheat shaped in cones;
      the circus man wages his bet. A mute girl in a freckled dress
         meandering
      down a canal of red-painted huts.

You never mentioned that, but it is so—
      What are these fires burning
      in rice? she gestures to the boy by
      sandbanks of a nearby creek. The one-eyed one tired by dusk
         & ready to end the question of birth & death.

Where do these trees come from? she squawks like the crows & only
      the ghostwoman, humming from the other side, hears.
      Chants off stream over mud ditches and fallen hats.

The singer already dead,
not the old ghostwoman's cooing by rice paddies.

This is what we find.

Taking off a tattered dress worn by the dead and dancing in mud the girl glanced over the snows of an empty field—the horse stood by the edge of a cliff and the voices circling about their wandering. All of this time she had thought that she & the boy were following them, that there was some purpose & destiny in their pilgrimage, and now she sensed in the night that we were following her here in night, she & the boy trailed by monks & ghosts & birds & trees & all of the others, and in that moment in a perfect silent pitch—*we are here*.

Dialogue XIII
> codes of emptiness

…languages of the unspoken then?
> --not beyond our translation.

When I was a boy you heard its alphabet in the brush by a train?

Now in a time of return.

I'd like to remember.

For the many who are first shall become last.

There is nothing said that is not unsaid?

Her walking by a ravine with transistor radio & uncombed hair.

When he finds he will be troubled and when he has been troubled, he
> will marvel.

Where now?

Black water eddies along the shore.

Have you discovered the beginning so that you inquire about the
> end?

Dialogue XIV
      draft sequences in a girl's diary

That you were living in a question brought
the sea, and later pelicans to shore, a boy &

      monk of a ghost sharing a bowl of tea. Curious
      a book on the dock by water might suggest

a girl's daily life, first
speech & sentences:

later, the draft sequences found in a
diary and even later, still, in the missing eye
of a boy. My mother

wanted to introduce herself in a
letter such as
pebbles to air, hawks & bluebird overheard

in nets cast over boats
awaiting a flurry of epistles

the boy might read. A way of saying it outside
myself she began, observing the boy's
kneeling over ants & beetles then without any
hesitation, throwing himself into a blush of blue water,
where all she could hear

afterwards was laughter.

This is what she had written & now reads to us.

Dialogue XV
     a boy's face before he was born

...walking quietly out of a room is enough at dawn.
     Waiting behind a plum tree,
& that morning he tricked his way into her speaking
     & what does it mean, following a procession of sounds from
a tongue she asks the boy who merrily merrily sings
in an oak grove;
skinny light out among seaweed on bay
where monastery bells echo out of gate
and I have come to find our family
though it is true you are free here,
this mute girl calls, longing for a boy's face before he was born.

Dialogue XVI
> our own trees, the girl says to her diary

In the line of death we see our own trees
of no coming & going, white cranes of appetite
ushering in monks' clothes & here
among river & precipice the ghostwoman has no place
or blame of killing, just ash
from a flame by water & our mutual
children sing a hymn from another
war, time itself shifting inward as a one-eyed
boy & mute girl traipse across the scene
themselves imagining a stage & hovering
in the absolute—what if in these birds rising,
the water also rises & nothing sings back
but the empty sound of no more shame.

A mute girl cawing in a wilderness.

A one-eyed boy seeing through the patience of a stone on a hill.

Who could blame or name or not hear
the inanimate speaking
through their wounded silence.

Dialogue XVII
     the ghostwoman replies

…only when you are you do we see two figures sauntering by cliffs
    overlooking a gorge.
The way a boy holds a favored hand.
       A green house among birch, an island where the ghost-boats
         once harbored us.
An aperture to sea & inside a body what is a word if not in the
    vanishing of boats,
even when the mute girl mouths *I love you,*
      the boy trips into clouds of unknowing.

     & each has to tell of their own it is so, yes, because only
     here is there is no more death.

The boy translates to the girl leaving his mother's grave—

>The monk passing by outside our window into the
>>water.
>You almost missed him? she asks.
>The funny thing is that he was right here.
>Not knowing is most intimate,
>不知道最爽, he wrote with his fingers on the moist
>>window panes,
>showing her the still
>visible handwriting above
>their bed of leaves.

Invisible river.

If you were a word in the house of language, what would you do the girl gestures towards little falcons into this tomorrow of naming the book: who I am listen. If only listening you will hear the end of story & tales by bones of our master. Where would you go if you were an I in a story and the story only gave you one word? The stillness of dawn at night, leaving home the boy utters and this conversation suggests a house where they lived as he leans squarely into her shoulders.

Dialogue XVIII
> a basket in a legend

The terraced hillside,
rice on tongue.
The dead one on a jagged side of her speaking.
Lit the lanterns for you, and incense for mother & brother & father, he
    says.
Why do you not fear death?
The circus master waltzes to the one great death: moon, mouth,
    morning.
We have not seen you dead.
Still, for the homeless, everywhere is home.
Playing cards with the dead?
You think death is a character of language.
The character of language is only blue, or earth, or a basket in a
    legend.
The one-eyed boy standing by his mother.
It is the dream where he breathes with both eyes.
A village of rectangular bones surrounding patches of lush green
    grass by creek.
A bridge heading into springs under mountains & rain.
We both die and never die.
I saw the death and unknew it.
There is a pond of lilies & mounds of dry earth, I'll take you there.
> The mute girl signaling above trees.

Dialogue XIX
        a forgotten people & time

…there were days on the river when we were floating on the raft of a
    book.
The girl was unborn?
The leaves began to fall,
albino crows following along shore.
Nostalgia & wanting, seared by a brightness not unlike my crow.
I was imagining you when I first entered their story.
Gooseberry & brush behind our house.
How long were you waiting?
 The raft of the book on a winter river drew us together.
And snow on banks one evening—& children huddled by fires with
    radios. Monks & soldiers roaming the roads.
The book inside a girl's story.
A forgotten people & time.
Light footsteps—unknowable water.
Still, you saw others, almost human, abiding.
Later egrets, even swans returned.
Pain outside the pain of love?
On shore after history had fled and the abandoning of narrative.
We are a ghost?
What is a ghost if not a boat?
I am the one who carried you.
You came to the boat that night.
It is never too late.
A cypress tree.
Did you know the others floating down river, neither dead nor alive?
We are all and none of them.

Talking with you, she writes in her diary:
       Tonight, the girl hears the secret sufi &
       sacred ceremony of our sema—our listening of whirling
       dervishes shedding black
       robes into a blind spinning upward &
       stringed music & call to prayer rising & falling,
       like birds of appetite in an inexplicable speech
       of longing & no separation.

Dialogue XX
    the girl's diary, Jiuhuashan

Mist on the eaves of a gate. Two
fisherman wading cross stream in a dusted
place. Questioning who he might be the boy skips
through bails & rows of hay—*hi Mom*—earlier hearing
the dream of our own death. The verb into
nowhere is not vanquished. A rock-faced
village & water buffalo scattered
among dirt paths & swamp ground. Kiss me in
the forgotten way, I gestured to clouds & boy
imagining how I once lived in this
temple but forgot the sweet aspen carrying back
to the hermit nun we stayed with near a lake.
The ghostwoman was kind. Now in another
time I only have you & these forests &
swamps & rice along a forbidden road
my breathing, looking into
the rain at everyone not there, then mouthing
these garbled words again for sky & you (who are here now)—
it's when you get close to death that things become
interesting, and then kissing his torn mouth.

Dialogue XXI
trees where I once left them

The letter back from the boy in weeks
relevant to time learned from a girl's
diary & the hours in a film unforgotten
days of photographs & board games &
dialogues between the bees where I once
left them & now clouds passing
a sky so keen in arrival that observation
in a letter opens to the meeting of apples
on the table between them—all the moments
to come and redemptive stones in a glass
cup where the girl holds the tip of a rose
& these parables we call forth in an imagined
passage of days & boats on water.

A monk looking at bay
in a language of emptiness
everywhere I go is homeless
everywhere I go is home he says
returning to the master's death
& cave of beginnings.

The circus man at river—
>	*the nature of prayer:*
>	*acceptance.*
>	*Walking without intent*
>	*may be closer to prayer*
>	*than is petitioning.*

I don't have to prove my existence,
the girl whispers back,
I don't have to prove my nonexistence, either.

Dialogue XXII
        49 days after death

…the boy awaiting my arrival, rambles across
a body no longer dead wood—
& three magpies looming
in memory. A form that exists before
form, plants, spring, & solitary spring rain sheeted over
streets & a make-shift door into
wind & the cypress grove
of tiny bonfires churning
incense, a boy suddenly hears a tower
chime for the first time
& cold clarity of
hand as the girl startles his shoulder &
the hollow of sky comes down to meet them
in a final bloom no one else sees.

Dialogue XXIII
  hiding in a book

You walk into her story & see us standing in a wheat field?
Speckled ostrich eggs fallen in a summer sky.
This is not where I left them.
Acorns spread across our leaves in approaching pilgrimage along
    mountains & sea.
In a sense, imagination is not only thought.
        The ghostwoman with honey on her breath. You found her
            wandering there.
        The boy born to bring it to expression?
He could not see her except in halves, and she only hears him in
    gestures?
The pear tree by our cottage still holding cracked walnuts & shells.
 They are not looking for anything now.
Monks & soldiers in these cliffs, all passage.
And lizards along the summer horizon.
We hid their names in the book.
Still, you miss them.
It is a shyness really, like that of lovers, some feeling of contrition or
    violation.
Why do you bother to record our dialogues?

Standing behind a stone wall by the orchard of our own arrival.
You see?
White cranes on a sea.

53

Dialogue XXIV
        just the other day

What is it you want from death?
The story coming home.
Just the other day.
I was thinking that too.
Burnt grass near a quarry.
Speaking in this way
made me think of summer.
She loved you, yes.
Who is their story then?
They are no longer becoming.
Rawness of a kiss.
Raw performance of a mouth.
We are full of choices.

A kiss known to a word.
And you are here, here now.
Why go further?
If you have come this far, why stop now?

Dialogue XXV
      the inanimate & a ghosted monk

Your nearness unfolding,
tracing lines of sounds in
an older language— *yuán fèn* & the boy
understood
a calling further back in
weeds wet with dew where they slept outside the walls
of a monastic city. The girl remembered
how, remembered the remembering
of that which cannot be touched
and only seen in an unseeing, here, in
an inanimate trace of our nearness
she whispers with fingers
as three water
buffalo appear through the morning dark
of earlier passage on a ridge west
to the place past rivers they again would walk
together in the written, though no longer alone.

It was in hindsight and always the monk walking that she came forward toward pause & blush of gratitude when she stepped over a puddle. The air cool, cucumbers & crickets in the phosphorus damp caves. The one-eyed boy watching her wrists take hold of a shirt, her thin legs shivering as the poet & circus man rode up on   bicycles. A monk brought pears. All these years to again meet—the ghostwoman sitting by bank, unfolding a scarf, the dead ones, too, the first to take the fruit offered.

Dialogue XXVI
      you too have been written

How could we harm them?
Their world is not finished.
When we left them in emptiness
their forms dreamed into us—
apple blossom that afternoon
in spring when you & your brother were playing and the war began.
They were holding hands.
Love & ravage.
A flight of redbirds over there to the west—follow my hand her
      striped blouse & the picnic & his offering.
You were surprised to discover them alive?
The two sleeping now. Stones on ground & in trenches by the cottage
      the boy & girl built before winter.
Never a chance to say goodbye?
Banyan & sidewalks. Black ants over cliffs, the angel there.
Go. You will find they, too, have been waiting.

Dialogue XXVII
    blood on snow

...all this time wandering, the girl says, looking
over a gorge where the one-eyed boy
had again written her. Because you come from it,
you will go there again. Sheered boulders &
drops, a wooden bridge in wind over
dry earth lined & red, red apple trees.
The coming home looks like this too, the girl ducks
into his neck.
When will you repose of the dead?
The sycamore & maple, nothing,
the key passage & no gain among
fish in streams reading back & out of time. When
I was last here, the moon was
blood in the fields. The mute girl
waving her arms, whisking away syllables she
could not pronounce as shapes
& shadows. We can die here &
live forever, the boy says it for her & now
the hermit nun's crooked mouth with no teeth.
They are like little children who
have installed themselves in a field?
Why not, the dead one trailing behind along
a brick path playing in the palm of my hands
even before they came into being.

Dialogue XXVIII
> three cranes fly off

Why are there always ghosts?
All night & all day, meandering in where she was written.
Scarecrows behind the remains of a monastery.
Is that where you first found her?
You make it alive.
But how does one love a story?
Stand at the beginning.
Finches lingering on limbs of the manzanita & madrone.
Is that when you were walking?
When she said i love you.
It was a day in the life of snow.
You make eyes in place of an eye?
She found this whenever she heard the meaning of her life.
Three cranes fly off.
No one lights a lamp & puts it under a bushel.
> When the three egrets flew off the river.
>> Why was she still trying to go home?
>> There were leaves in the tracks along the water.
>> An owl waiting.
Did the boy know?
Empty they have come into the world, empty they seek to go out
again.
The boy was ready to discuss all the signs. He sensed they were no
longer and she was ready, yes.

Dialogue XXIX
      everything you always wanted

The boy walking backwards in a noon
hat & pebbles off a road tossing up
with bare feet a current riveting into
a window outside attention where
the only breeze in days falls back & gulls
come by Haliç waters & then you see your only
life & stumble into their room not
knowing a story's child & where it goes
after lamps come on as a boy looks downward
and a swarm of wasp buzz off eastward,
a cat scooting under a small moored
boat, and the saddling of a horse
and blue tile of a tekke and this silence of a veiled
girl's carrying rope to market in a minaret's
sounding only a moment ago while a man
stooped by the shop near a mosque's window
& a green leaf & her mute smile &
everything you always wanted you already are,
she stutters, again, and the boy's own calling home
in a voice of the girl's
throat as if leaning into speech or learning to
speak all over again while covering
her hair with his eye in an unspoken rain.

Dialogue XXX
> to the reader

...standing at the sixth ancestor's gate?
> Are you enlightened? a girl asks Master Hui Neng, watching
> blind monks cross over stream.

The black crust of coal, washed bare feet.
> Inside the question again the girl appears astonished?

No longer abiding in blame, the muted ones herd her hands
> as water buffalo begin to arrive,
> and the ghostwoman foregoes a dance.

So many days of sitting, our ghostedness not even a ghost.

Falling into chanting & walking, a one-eyed boy spots a drop of blood
> on stone.
> What self to be enlightened, the girl calls forward,
> answering her own question
> while all of these visions vanish in water.

Just the thought is already us.

Dialogue XXXI
 memory of passage

Mud on cobblestone & sharp-edged
sway of mountains & at knife point:
a hut above poverty & red dust.
All these children in the rain. Buses &
forbidden language, the mother
drifting upward surrounded in
shrouded lamps & shingle-tiled brick stone.
Houses strewn with trash;
we arrive on rickshaws & motorcycles—
a one-eyed boy in a village trailing his father
through rice paddies calling out
who are you, Manjushri.
looking up from soil. Yes, where am i & who
are you, the circus man inquires. All leaves float up in a
weave of cool air. A perfect autumn day
& three wild geese trace a canal: a flight
then, thatched roofs floating around shafts
of bamboo & jagged roads. A girl
looks back, a clear lake as they see
each other & a quiet over toads
& cattails & caterpillars & hey scarecrow
she says, are there others like us in these hills?

A naming?
Yes, the story is not a face but the face is God.
They walked on together as if in stillness,
 coming forth from unknown handwriting.

In a line of movement along a road the miraculous & these things however it meets you. What might it ask (in need) of you, lover or friend. Bowed their heads & stronger now in attention: insects & vegetables in a garden. With my mouth I remember. A former house of language. The sentence asking tender mercy arrives alone. All these years & narratives, the girl caws—sounding of wind on fire. It was like this in her garments. An embrace of body. The plants & proc-lamations & ending of time.

Dialogue XXXII
      grasshoppers & snow

Figs from thistles, grapes from thorns.
The girl wets her lips below a window
above pigeon eaves— if you come from it
and become a passerby, a life approaching its own
untelling.

        A vine has been planted,
        my circus man sighs,
        that's love.

And so the four of us enter yet another embarkation.
If no death is the place, there is no gate,
& who calls down into bamboo—sensing no one
but an eye & ear in wood—if not this chafed knowing,
what is there in our vast unknowing,

        stumbling across a bridge to the south hill,
        carrying a bucket
        on this crisp cold winter morning.
        The empty theater etched over
        grasshoppers & snow.

Is it impossible for a boy to mount two horses,
or a girl to stretch two bows?

And so a movement & rest:
freckled shoulder, offering a
carving of a foot from her left hand.
Because when you come from it,
you go there again.

Dialogue XXXIII
    hey there, hey radio

...unsounded in a story of fields. Footprints over words.
A girl observing one wing
by stone—and always the same unfurling
of green leaves: physical body, fleeting
liftings, a found place, temple &
the 84,000 gates past a mother
& father of the girl's early studies;
careening home, wind
in from the Gobi Desert
(beyond Dragon Gate, she whispers).
Here, see, she mouths, in return—
markets of watermelon & sun, kale, & pink
round oranges. A mute child in a red sweater
on a bicycle. *Hey there.* Birch & linden trees by
smoke off factory pipes by railroad tracks.

            —dragons live out beyond
            the mouth,
            a monk calls back passing two crooked river bends—

Now a passage between language & caves
and why are these hills in the shape
of a sea? the girl asks.
Corn on a clothes line. Rice on terrace.
A boy watching & studied:
 Or refuges coming & going this time

of year, why sleep? The girl finding
speech a rather unsophisticated
& dubious matter. Edges of birth,
 a precipice & big leap—the mountain
with all of them, the monks tell her.
Whoever finds explanation will not taste death.

Dialogue XXXIV
    crumbling walls of a city

This always coming back to a beginning
where there are no names in the speaking &
a girl tiptoeing in on the way we first
loved when we went out on the road,
and Tower of Galata & Blue Mosque & bending
white guitars, breath as language & unknown blizzard &
buzzard drifting over Bosphorus and a girl's voice
issuing up in a quiet, furtive blinking &
boats that bring the eye to its own unseeing—
waves earlier that morning as the boy
lingered by shore & painted our image
of ourselves in himself and still past turquoise
gulf, fishermen & crumbling walls of a city
& reading inside the ruptured shifts of a clock
& scales from fish that trail her in & out
of oars & these unwritten letters home.

Dialogue XXXV
>not seen other than in its who

The boy on his way back into a wound,
brooked hills & books of afternoon rain over ants
the dead who they were phoning from a roadside bar,
who, as my bicycle man made his entrance,
swirled by the empty trash cans & emptying well
overlooking a sky—below from a gorge where all we
could smell were desert sands over emptiness &
oral ridges & between who the awe of gone
& who in their wings shifting across fine dust & water
a prayer chanted again reached up again & toward
who, a heart not seen other than in its who
& tear & split & angel who listened to the scene
by phone & turning pages from the book of events & studying
a fox & a boy's collapse into
a girl's grace & attention to unknowing.

Counting her fingers again in the forgotten way seeing the boy stand beside her ghost in a collaboration of notes & drawings as pebbles slipped from his hand into the ghostwoman's exploring a quality of an authentic withered beauty heard over the constant change in the girl's view of things, at last, as it is—just as it is & nothing perfect, nothing lasting & no thing unfinished.

Dialogue XXXVI
  the king of emptiness

...traipsing over a road to be one's own
in trees & tea & thin cuttings
of minarets, and maybe even winter sun
closing all trails & thinking of you on this crisp
cold morning before dawn,
a mute girl sleeping.
Aloneness herself tonight—these clothes,
this speech, this gesture—what you expect
has come.
A man traveling east & west—carved wooden
bridge crossing time a girl
glancing backward toward a boy one-eyed &
hovering by banks of gold & its stains.
What you expect has come, but
you dismiss the living before you
and speak of the dead,
our circus man laughs.
A veiled woman pulling a blue bucket
of damp abayas upward & along a brick wall.
A sufi on a bicycle peddling
baskets of octopus, shrimp,
prompt repulse & scavenger blood, the monk
asks, why yes, yes—if only we accepted ourselves,
who we are alone on a highway
tonight, a relinquished paradise.
A whiteness, scored

light & music of windows looking out
into jade of the straits, boats at moor
& a fisherman's
weeded rooftop &
call to prayer & fog & wash of snow, and
& fried oysters in a market. We reclaimed it
(the past). Or gabble of geese
in another ear, theness then of
dark within dark
night you shall enter
&—reconnaissance, rendezvous, recognition,
who hears on the day of harvest &
our own lives also appear, the mute
girl curls into an alley.
Who walks with his feet,
who sees with his hands?
Why it is you, a boy terrene
dragoman by banks.
Actuality of the actual under hills,
a whiteness scored in torn music,
mosques peering into
clustered water of bushweed
& red, red rooftops conducted along
a sloped horizon.

Yes, yes, thinking of you on this crisp cold
winter morning before dawn, she writes,
and in case you ever wondered if we love you.

Dialogue XXXVII
     the boat by her hair

Coming back to that place that sea that here
that is not here & the said unsaid
a one-eyed boy passing a café by foot
& a farfetched word mustered at last
in its give & take among the waters &
a blue cliff record & observation in the girl's
straw bag swinging on her shoulder
the way the unsaid said
all these stones & stories where are we
going the boy asks a mute girl stumbling
into our book in her torn skirt & tennis shoes
& the born unborn (ok) & the unusual
perspective of her eyes & thickening hair
might present to you some kind of problem
yet the day before our meeting
that this grew in the boy's own sense
of disorder to walk & wake here along a sea
on the edge of a boat & into the burning
of what really matters she says—wow,
a burning that matters.

Dialogue XXXVIII
  red leaf of autumn

…what if this were the first & last day of our birth?
the girl now mouths to the one-eyed boy climbing
backward in toward the hut of our final
speaking. In a story there is never a beginning
& end— whose voice traces itself in air while each
autumn goes crisp. To speak of love,
an untamed signature of words holds
no yesterday or tomorrow, the ghostwoman
says, pages falling in around
as she steps forward toward our heroes
hovering by the shadow
of her own mother's
photograph held up in one hand. But you keep
your foot next to the Buddha, she grins
uncounted moving past
so in this what you
say in birth is only an echo
of the nearness of death
unfolding inside & around us.

Watching blind monks
cross over streams
the boy spots a drop
of blood on stone.

Dialogue XXXIX
>the word now spoken

Who are you now?
The girl asked the boy this in the Book of the Floating Raft.
Not in the Book of Events?
Nor in the Book of Unknowing.
What is your story?
The legend behind you left in time.
Where are your people from? the girl asks now, walking beyond a
>white field.
(She stutters again passing by voices, like trees. The one-eyed boy
>once more seeing into the face of the albino deer on a ridge.)
A cadence of hair?
Three days, the light of a wing.
I saw you once in this way, the circus man laughs circling on his bicy-
cle in the parking lot.
All the gusts of leaves.
It was like this in her silence?
Vigorous wind. Tiptoeing roadsides, late sun, the hives of bees
>lingering in the shadows of others.
It was just like that, yes, the gaze she reached, one that later she
>would remember more than all the rest.
In a dream of language we begin.
Cypress & bamboo bending, a wooden water tower, a boy sitting in
>tall grass, reading her diary and the ghostwoman waving from a
>bridge.
As she listened she heard the shapes of letters in her mouth.
The words now speaking.

Dialogue XL
  a wandering word

…so the thing needed to say itself, stark color of leaves
    —all your life you had waited;
& acorns fallen by questions, what a field
might dream in others;
    —already in the wound, yes.
a study of seeing & a one-eyed boy going into whistles
not hearing minarets hearing now,
    (still here, to hear, an unending quiet);
& dialogues too of sun in morning sun
    —good talks with the dead—
when he finds he will be troubled—*hey there,*
you, and our last unsayings waking a body:
    (the book of the unwritten, it is time
    to return it. you are not it
    it is, in fact, you.)
green & filtered slopes furling outward
down seaward on inside out as a kiss.
once torn mouth, apples & ants,
settled stone, silt & solitude.
all the girl could gesture in flight while sands move
forwarding motions of waves in a hand imagining no
more war—*no, no, no,* she caws with a crow,
& just these final moments traipsing seaside,
an oyster bed & red rose
where all birds muster & flutter forth
    in praise of no one or one thing.

*

there were days on the river when we were
floating on the raft of a book.

*

whoever has ears to hear let him hear
            —a one-eyed boy speaking in a mute girl's unspoken
            mouth,
the memory of bees toward eves of harboring boats.
birch & bare fields.
a stumbling girl & awkward boy in woods;

silver fish set forth on the chopping block.

*

...or wings of ostrich and all you ever wanted to be.
say now, i don't know.
            —& i came to learn the source of their wandering.
who speaking in an unseen evening?
            —a sky & four horses & vast mountainside,
toy trains, and everything for you:
just for you. wood toy capital of the word,
            —walking into you there was only an echo,
crossings across ravage & lizard tracks.

*

what country are we in now?
she hums, a boy enters water,
pieces of prayer on matchsticks, the girl mouths in his
    ear,
toys are a scene seen everywhere, always.
hooray.

*

taking no thought from morning until evening
i was walking in figures
by bay & no more
turn aside.
this the place we have arrived in.
        ghosts & monks in greenside over there—
        (where?)
& windows of huts & curious rooms
keeping watch over this place
of no more vanishing.

a good thing, too.

*

that gorge surrounded by river & sea
& mist.

original face—
        entering the gap between where thought appears;
for three days he circled it,

reciting from the yangtze basin to the bosphorus & on
the trail of a nun to the caves at summit.

go on.

        —who chose this face for me?
a monastic field within an eye where all roads gather.

        *

...or the leafing of pine & oak hovering
below an eye: you make eyes in place of an eye?
      —while being lived we came to you early one morning.
& finely-veined stairs of a pagoda where the dead
leave their bodies before floating upward & visible in
bamboo wall of fish & dragon paintings'
final departure.
      —a small boat in an eddy,
      we saw a face & tale telling itself of no abode.

        *

tripping over a father's coat & three sticks of incense,
a boy smoked loose tobacco from the pocket & lit
a stubbed candle at the foot of a toy wooden soldier.
        The hermit-nun
wisped up beside him in frayed gray robes.
      —the nothing that is no longer separate here.
he offered one incense for his mother & the other
two for his father & brother.

—no longer or other or of imagined thing.

where we go is good enough by me.
love's final mystery.

*

the boy turned angling through tall fern,
and the ghostwoman pointed toward a track
of language a mute girl left scattered on the side
of a road 1000 years before.
      —you see her standing by a transistor radio and a red
          scooter.

but if we are dead and our world is finished,
 how is it her voice still exists, he asks?

*

if not in this, who?
tunneling into the back of a hand & a circus master's
quarters, whispers under bridge & a central blood
line narrative of red earth.

      —both ways of a road appear?
      not a thing or sentence but what we have become.

you could say that.
      —story & breath, two figures pausing to read by a sea.
& by the way: magnolia now to his left;

83

those bushy yellow flowers of osthmanthus
to the right of albino deer.
a one-eyed boy's green lizard
crawls across the girl's diary.

*

so you discovered the beginning &
you inquire about the end?

it was a final hour under elm & honeysuckle.
       —you are not dead,
       the ghostwoman calls out at dawn, and in this way
we arrive back at the beginning—
and resume the work.

*

       my mouth will not at all be capable.
       a girl hears the fish speaking & guesses it is the hour
       stroking a grasshopper over his mouth.

*

a hand turned outward & our drunken sister's wandering—
a sheer apple, black butterfly & spoken grass,
melon on a wooden table: dragoman taking you

into black water eddies along a cradle
    (our girl sung them yes she did).

84

the way we tethered inside a mother's passing years later.
      —you were between deaths,
      reading from the book of events.
ears populated in pages & sandpipers all up & down shore.
 always half-open, his eye.
      —a boy shed her exhale a final breath & now another
sequel to the astonished.
but where now?
      —stars plunging over horizon. moments.
      yet you have been here before.

*

signals & signs & bluebirds & lines, porcupines & pines,
homeless (again) reading backwards from a railroad station,
—bye bye, papa—
while brushing aside.
      —you thought this was a secret of your own life,
      & so it is so: mixing up the table of contents wherever he
        walked.
not quite ready for a game of hide & seek, the girl in a stream under
    cormorant in search of a tune.
whose wound?

*

suitcases & stairs going toward squirrels & bears,
    alphabets of tea & leaf—
& all this for you.

who smells the workings of a fabulous world?
that's a good question.
becoming passers-by & figs from thistles
& grapes from thorns.

a girl becoming a passage?
         —in the other ear, yes—
the sound of her muteness
when she said i love you.
a mother glancing back & forth in all these roadside
exaltations.
popcorn & coca colas at the movies tonight.
no commercials?
right you are.
     a handless monk saying—awesome curl of her toe into a
        weeping willow, not unlike this, (look) to a boy in flight
        through burning bees.

i was looking for my father, the boy says.
and all of this time, here you are.

some ghosts seem skittish around here.
blind men crossing blind man's bluff.

(a father leaning when i saw him at a final
station waving good-bye.)
the circus man at the edge of a highway.
a mute girl carrying strawberries along the tracks.
radio o radio.
coaxing silence out of noiseless weeds.
(you better cut that.)
        —no one lights a lamp & puts it under a bushel;
it was winter & we received a sky.
what else did she say?
        —a wandering girl in a plaid skirt playing hip hop
        on the skin of a drum.

*

words & redbirds keep & giving you the slip?
        beings & non beings of noon & obliterated beauty
        awake & awaiting & arriving on a cypress stump.
they (who now?) changed the names of a story
because this is only no death:
        silt at stream bottom, the boy's empty tin can
        dancing & ablutions on shore.
layer & layer of weed & dirt & faces washed in cloud & camp light.
what else?
we are only our own dream in
a movie on a slow-moving train in a show of white geese descending
on grassy banks.
        (& even the dream dreaming.)
        *

you're confused, perhaps that's it?
only so that his eyes will not be broken.

*

do the generals miss their mothers?
the girl with
        a raggedy-ann doll asks the dead one.
...wars taking no thought from morning to evening.
how could we forget them?
the dead not even dead,
history a house with no home.
i saw,
saw?

*

        the sky grey shape of cranes coming inward in wind
        & world & word from sea.

*

the townspeople from these ridges,
a girl cawing in the ears of corn gathering round our muted mouths.
lotus & rice paddies too
                —the things around hear & pronounce their shape.
meadows over canals on this horizontal plane—& now:
            touch of a mistranslation that is only.
whereas in a dream of language we have no regret or longing.
why did you allow the killing?

she asks the general staggering in her footsteps by a canyon.
            —it is impossible for a man to mount two horses.

*

        your nearness is all
        nearsighted magpie, pear blossom
        swan & egret, & fecund
        blue earth of unsaid things.

*

rain on cobblestone, red brick to sea.
rainbows & lollypops & who you won't see.
that's the way it is.

*

only moments ago, yes
the boy responds as they walk into words,
looking eye to eye in the face of god.

*

in stillness your nearness is all.
            —this is where the prayer comes from
            as we stand back in sounds that are no longer
            and never were our own.
                    *

a one-eyed boy pretends to be a soul.
why *pretends?*
                    —we are not & not only here.
a child keening by a watering hole.
why not?
who are you, spotted birch tree?
white dragon mountain—you ain't kidding nobody;
dragon spring river—roll your waters this way;
flowing cloud creek tributary—lots of us here;
cave palace mountain range where we said goodbye—
only names.
                    (the girl calls back with the call
                    to prayer and the birds fly up.)

                              *

i was playing cards with my card playing man.
evening prayer by minaret.
just lit the lanterns for you
& all the walkers,
and incense, again—
& you, always you:
leaves away & into these cypress trees webbing along
branches of bush.
          the funny thing is the ancestors are
stones & walls too.
              they speak with their ear
              in drifting books of eaves
              all these years of soft elm in a
              conference of birds talking to you:

one might be passing outside
your window.
hi, she says.

*

they love the tree & hate the fruit,
or they love the fruit & hate its tree.
the found noun becomes a sovereign,
this beginning born into remembering
& forgetting.

*

figures of syllables & parable
pause between words.

*

thanks, man.

*

characters of speech traipse
in cups of wine
& loaves of bread.

*

what you find is not a ghost but a blooded
song.

> —now we too have passed thru the place they paused in
> the book.

*

each has to tell of their own
birth & death.
> —an island that once harbored us before we began.

*

482 A.D.
the general tells a story of a temple's
burning over 1500 years ago. among deaf trees
a boy squinting
one-eyed, the elders all merging in *our vanishing*.
the lines on a piece of paper.
> (until he eyed her by the circus master's grave.)
> until we meet again, yes.

*

> still, quiet sky, waves, still,
> remembering of water as it
> remembers itself.

*

not knowing a small wave in the middle of seeing.

*

i want to learn something from you,
the girl says:
why did you become a monk anyway?
were you just bored?

*

i am not afraid of your death, she says.
you are now written here.

*

when you were dead these were fragments
of bird & word left from the sky,
the boy tells her.

*

small sufi village near where
the mute one lived as a child now
            ashore
            by byzantine ruins & lycian burial grounds.
pointing his nose out behind a rock face,
            the circus man begins to talk.

*

how to live—
all eyes on all things inside messenger fields.

*

and so the story goes on and leaves you.
i see no one or one thing, she says.

*

the slow growth & change of rite & religious dogma—
& shade of a homeless
man squatting under bridge over there
surrounded by motorcycles & rickshaws.

these fires burning in rice &
the end of the question of birth & death,
a language of the unspoken,
black water eddies along shore.

*

that's manjushri, the girl salutes, hand
over hand over mouth over hand,
an alphabet without desire.

*

that you are living in a question brought the shadow grass,
my diary & all lost in war,

94

awaiting a flurry of epistles,
in fishing nets cast over shore.

*

i was thinking of you in the morning:
a drop of blood on the blade
over a heart:
to endure.

*

train pulling into a station
here the children head south on bicycles.
where did they all come from?
she asks the boy
wandering among pebbles
of a river.
    —this is what she writes & reads to him
    kneeling over waves without any hesitation.

*

the countryside scattered with abandoned
factories, concrete blocks grown over with bush
& trash, a drop of blood on a blade over heart:
go on.

    —a mute girl longing for a boy's face before
    he was born.

*

the ghostwoman, too, blown back by these
bright moon-shaped faces
& confessions,
and the dead come about.
                         a sun beating down
in the thrust of winter.
whose face is that, she asks—
skinny legs edge out among seaweed
on a stormed over oyster bay;
hermit nun & monk
with them in the book of events.
                    the mind gaining feeling, a flavor
of salt in the character.
                    looking over a talus in snow.
the eyes of a child
knitted in a plum tree.

*

i would cut off
my arm, too, to end their suffering.

in the line of death we see our own trees,
of no coming & going,
white cranes of appetite.

*

you don't have
an arm to spare, the girl says.

*

back at the monastery (here)
no place of blame:
the soldier killed his teacher: the landscape shifting as
                huts & villagers come out to meet
us.
our own lives closing in around
love.
nothing is tangible, the ghostwoman utters in
the girl's ear.
only when you are you is it the whole works.
            —they do not put new wine into old wine skins.
two figures sauntering by cliffs overlooking a canyon.

*

or words written on a mouth?

*

this is your liberation. even
eaves & falls, hills & rocks,
                trees & city walls, palaces…
                why, only yesterday we were hardly breathing.
dust into green fields & vegetables
& untouched hands.

—like crawling head & all into a roll your own smoke?
we both die and never die.

days floating down river on the raft of a book.

a river called we always meet
pages fallen along shells,
blush water pushing up against horse &
red-hued barges & ferris wheel &
skyscrapers going bye-bye, blackbird.
bye-bye.

a monk, called by the name empty cloud,
boning marrow every three
steps,
       bowing his way up countryside, 1500 miles of
       bowing every third step,
a mute girl carrying his bowl.

when empty cloud walked into the general's
quarters beside her, one thousand friends suddenly rose up
in tattered soldiers' uniforms.

i told you to come alone, the general stammered,
looking about at their faces.

these are the dead, your dead, monk empty cloud says,
taking hold of her hand—
                    all the same,
                    a stone a stone,
                    a vow a vow,
& to meet in this auspicious way she mouths
to the one who resembles her father.

                              *

pigeons & crickets all the way to the capital
letters of no separation.
                    walking into words there was only an echo.

                              *

stretching into nothingness
the inanimate speaks.

                              *

is there anything here?
                    —the calm rain in sleep.

*

who is in the place where you are going?

*

chao chao is still here.
stones carrying lives inanimate, still here.
read by lanterns & all embrace, still here.
butterfly lovers in west lake swimming, still here.
human too
because a mute girl, a one-eyed boy
decided to spend morning & evening with birds, still here.
the table where you sat, still here.
a smooth place to place a hand, still here.

*

well if you say so.

*

now that death is near, I choose to live.

*

why don't you ask our name?

*

the circus master bows to the unborn.

*

when the girl looked into the mirror
mirror mirror on the wall
she saw the thingness of things.
          (if it were a name, you'd be trapped by it.)

*

the way verbs cry?
          —entering where the gap between thoughts appear.
the muteness of nouns too, yes.

the loneness, and an emperor in a purple
robe & monkeys in bamboo.
          —no longer of other or imagined thing.

*

what is a city then, you inquire:
          —story & breath, two figures pausing to read by sea;
as they trail along the frontier sound
& sentences stirred in tea.
a boat toward her
          —if not in this, who?
sipping his cup
a boy becomes amazed.
          yes, where else, if not here?

who else (where now) if not here.

*

(don't forget this part)
a thumbless woman playing poker by the truck stop.
the king understanding your death.
            we had been here before
            in a final hour under elm & honeysuckle.

*

hermit caw mute girl
            something that had brought the girl again, yes.

*

mirror mirror on the wall
who is the who of us all?

*

the boy in his wool coat flying
            —we saw the one-eyed boy, yes—a boat builder,
            a fisherman helping & seals all about:
when you touch the unsaying it says
the unsaid, a one-eyed face
kissing your wound.

*

when will you repose of the dead?
a girl hems the cloth of fish speaking
& guesses it is the hour.

*

all of my friends died & reborn here.
      —you were between deaths?
the art of war no war, she again mouths the words
toward a movement & a rest.
       —the boy playing cards by the docks of a bardo.

you can say that again.

*

studying the events.

*

on the road again
a mistress from a secret morning swoons:

    (thus, the ghostwoman told him)

red tiled roofs.
so many human passages.
what makes a person dead or alive?
      small shells & husks of shells, this i can attest to.

*

happy birthday, papa—
you're 55 & still alive.

*

water buffalo grazing in rice paddies earlier,
ducks in a duck pond.
                —as if it were the last thing.

*

pebbles of astonishment.
                —this was the first thing she said to the boy, yes.

*

not i or you or
or

*

                    a tattered girl & a red scooter,
                    (a black & orange t-shirt)
                    running down the middle of a highway
                    with a transistor radio.

i saw.
saw?

*

the unlined margins of water.

*

the vocabulary of her father.

*

cormorant, pipers, reserved letters, signs.
            —you made it alive, pissing up & down this road.

*

just this mediation of haystacks
            —before we even heard them in a wave.
            where a light originated through itself—
(*the sounds of muteness*
when he said it).

a father washing his children
in the middle of a lake.

on one side of shore, hushed
shoots, a mute girl, red peppers in
a rusty stove; on the other side, ravage
of saying who you are like.

            —because when you come from it, you go there again.

*

if the father eats too much salt,
the son drinks a lot of water.

*

and a red wheelbarrow of marbles being hoisted
up an apartment building by a sufi mason.

(we sensed they would arrive
with the deepening of winter.)

ah, and here gardens along twigs,

ah, a row of corn stalks at the frame
of a former painting of you, stalking brush
& ah, yellow-tailed dragons.
                    —it was winter and we were studying a sky.

*

huineng's refuge rock—
          i saw you there.

across from nanhau temple
               —the mute girl carrying a bucket full
               of strawberries along
               an ashen wall.

jealous monks pursuing him set mountains on fire
　　　　　　—that was the first time she
　　　　　heard us with her own ears.

wooden bridge over tsaohi river
　　　　　opposite the leaning beams.

　　　　　　　　　　*

i remember that.
　　　　　i heard you there.
it was winter and we were looking for a sky.

　　　　　　　　　　*

note:
come back to handwriting: "animate/
inanimate as well as next
epistle
　　　　　　—language is a place, the burning fields,
　　　　　the story never leaves you, & ps
　　　　　your life is only a dream....

　　　　　　　　　　*

found, fine, find, nina.
"i'm fine, you're great."
stand at the beginning.

　　　　　—the story is not only you.

banyan trees to the south
of pearl river.

      —here. this is the coat that was your father's.
      now it is yours.

      *

i was having a smoke outside the theater:
& you said i will walk with you.
molten cliffs in sharp
crevices, the shape of knuckles,
sycamores slip away
banyan webbing along the rough
gray branches unfolding
as hedges in air.

you should have seen it.

      —is that why you have come?

      *

rain & ran, sand & eyelashes.
do you want to see the two ancient problems?
      (so his eyes will not be broken.)
i say it is hard to find someone who knows
shame & consciousness.
      —we have no regrets or longing, the girl says.

fertile in which 'i am' is always dead:
rice drying on a freeway,
a woman raking a yard by a mute girl.
                    —treetops hovering above a village.

(i love seeing rice coming into non-being, too.)

                            *

and so on a word wandering,
toward the end of a word in
orange or brown meadows, pinkish hills;
            —the sky gray shape of cranes;
human soliloquies every life time;
            —the things around here pronounce their shapes.

                        *

hanging clothes on a clothes line;
                —there is no longer the same moon,
                the same river, the same cloud.

no need to kill or be killed.

                        *

release us to our fields.

—a nomenclature or a mouth?
or simply vegetation blooming up wind winding
inside & outside time;
or neutral space, bird seed & saddling in
the way horses always come round.
      —where is there room for yes or no?
is that what you've been trying to say?

      —a fierce wind in the mountain only a moment ago.

*

in her diary:
(i have an idea followed by a question, if you are listening?)

…among the harmless—
wild stranger & spirit of dispossession,
love that bowl of soup,
          a face outward

leaves this world every few
words or so.

*

      the hermit coughs over
fecund blue earth of once ordered things
and the aboutness
        (without fear?)

—the boy asks as we walk toward them.

*

we are this hereness in our all.

*

stand back in sounds that are no longer
& never were our own.

*

we're leaving.
where to? she says.
        —the mute girl looks over the walls of a city.
a moon & bus home & who are who you are.
maple. camphor. magnolia. osmanthus:

i can understand that.

*

i've drank my fair share of wine—
        but where does the stillness come from?

*

you want something definite, but i prefer
something indefinite, she sighs

when he kisses her mouth.

*

      —the girl puts her sandal in the one-eyed boy's
      hand and tiptoes to shore,
      imagining he is a boat.

*

on the day of harvest the weeds appear.
language shifting in her mouth.
a boy swimming in summer.

*

but what & who is that girl?
nothing ever really happens.

      —all the people who lived here.

*

my bicycle man falling into the brightness of leaves.
a finer voice that day?
you could say that,
      and a solitary one, too.

*

you who make safe in the dark,

112

thank you.
       to look in the same direction.

*

rain, rain, & rain coming down on the pagoda tonight,
the sky restless.
       a hermit walking down tracks
by rusted lampposts,
& over there, huts, a leaf. awesome.
         (the egret in a creek, ta ta,
         humming and we step back.)

*

(still, some ask for a more suitable translation.)
and this beginning:
born into always beginning.

*

a shadow on water of fishermen
emptying nets by bay
& feeding gulls.
        that's clear enough.

*

the illness of a train is culture, she writes in a diary
by a herd of goats.

...hills of human earth flickering
over history & going on.
      —the circus man studying paleography.
& watershed basins,
        & as for ourself, the silence of language most cherished.

        *

...it was always you
in a wildness,
by oyster bed by bay;
     anyway, i just came up here
to say thank you

        *

& anyway, as tired as you probably are
       (who she is, yes)
nothing to seek
of things.

        *

     —once we believed in a story
       we saw ourselves also vanishing in:
crest of sparrows
crows down river
ridge &
languages
behind minarets

in an open field.

*

when i was a boy an effervescent here
among deer & horses,
       & throughout draft sequences in a diary

a girl's version of daily life:
mules by mosque & monastery.
       (& the boy written here & at home,
       she says, taking hold of his face.)

*

fishing nets cast over boats,
          (only the boy might read)
walking quietly across the room
that lifts by
hand along muddy water

in a bright tone of being.

*

a girl crying out
at breakfast—hooray,
a boy seeing through
a hill in the dark—
the mute girl signaling above trees.

*

who could blame
or name
or not hear
the inanimate
speaking through
their wounded silence?

Acknowledgements

Dialogue I, a source of their wandering (for Nina Simone)

Dialogue II, a girl of familiar kiss (for Karen Russell)

Dialogue III, the mute girls asks (for Murat & Karen Nemet-Nejat)

Dialogue IV, at the end of a word (for Forrest Gander)

Dialogue V, language shifting in her mouth (for Fanny Howe)

Dialogue VI, the ghostwoman & a game of soccer (for Baz & Martha King)

Dialogue X, a boy and a bottom well (for Lisa Bourbeau)

Dialogue XI, mending nets offshore (for Blanche & Lou Hartman)

Dialogue XII, questions of birth (for Maria Zhao)

Dialogue XIII, codes of emptiness (for Susan & David Frankel)

Dialogue XIV, draft sequences in a diary (for Ancient Path)

Dialogue XV, a boy's face before he was born (for Handan Arikan & Ravza Kızıltuğ)

Dialogue XVI, our own trees, the girl says to her diary (for Patricia Pruitt & Chris Sawyer-Lauçanno)

Dialogue XVII the ghostwoman replies (for Claire Libin & Bob de Silva)

Dialogue XVIII, a basket in a legend (for Trav, Milah, Mindy, & Chaz)

Dialogue XIX, a forgotten people & time (for Joe Donahue)

Dialogue XXI, trees where I once left them (for Sasha)

Dialogue XXII, 49 days after death (for Chao Chao)

Dialogue XXIII, hiding in a book (for Bo Bo, aka Tim Chen)

Dialogue XXV, the inanimate & a ghosted monk (for Zhang Er, Leonard Schwartz, and Cleo)

Dialogue XXVI, you too have been written (for Omer Çolakoğlu)

Dialogue XXVII, blood on snow (for Huike)

Comments on John High's *here* and *a book of unknowing*, the first two books in the trilogy:

a book of unknowing:

"Imagine a novel whose setting is dark and indeterminate, whose nameless characters are shadowy, and whose circular plot unfolds timelessly — and you will be imagining John High's *a book of unknowing*. These powerful poems, whose language rushes past in a torrent of disorienting yet evocative images and sounds, will pull you out of this world and into another, that matters a great deal more, where all that you think you know becomes doubtful." —*Norman Fischer*

"John High's poems, threaded together by narratives of childhood that span a century, are always immediate, grounded, and as fleeting as the moment. Throughout, High's art stays close to the heart. The music is visible." —*Matvei Yankelevich*

here:

"This book — and it really is a Book — walks the paradoxical intersection back and forth — between substance and spirit — with restless, spare steps. Fleeting images of the monastic life — as an assurance and a dream — can't quite dissolve the secular disappointments and losses behind each sentence. This way the book becomes for the reader what it is for the writer: a searing study of Here as an enfolded Everywhere." —*Fanny Howe*

"In *here* John High has created a cinema of the page Tarkovsky himself might treasure. This book-length elegy for a brother is also a gathering of icons for the end of the world, a world of nostalgia and sacrifice and unremitting vision, the 'normal grandeur of abandon,' the poet might let slip, as his extraordinary scenes float before us. Blood, snow, branches, a one-eyed boy, questions for an empty sky, all flare in this film, this pilgrimage to a place, here, that seems, after all, as death sometimes does, to be traveling as well towards us. It would be too cruel to say this book is one John High was born to write. Let s just say: how lucky the dead man was, to have been so loved." —*Joseph Donahue*

"In this book-length elegy rendered in the sparest strokes, the silence of the dead meets a Zen stillness centered in the author's own practice. John High handles his subject with the most delicate distance — we never fully see the brother he mourns, but we sense him always, getting larger and larger, as only the dead can do, until he has become indistinguishable from the world he left. In this lovely book, High turns elegy to discovery while retaining the truth of sadness, and matches brevity with a generosity that not only grasps, but also loves, the human condition." —*Cole Swensen*

"Reading this poem, we become aware of the 'leaves and ghosts of leaves,' crows, jays, tulips, lilacs and rain. Writing the natural world begins and ends with a 'vanishing out here among us.' And time, the 'empty boat,' implies the emptiness that is form. John High's lucid and compassionate text is threaded through with photographs taken by poet and Zen priest Norman Fischer." —*Norma Cole*

The author:

John High ranks among the most accomplished and respected poets, translators, and editors of his generation. Founding editor of *Five Fingers Review* and author of *the lives of Thomas, The Sasha Poems, The Desire Notebooks, Bloodline: Selected Writings,* here, and *a book of unknowing,* among others, he is one of his generation's foremost translators of contemporary Russian poetry. The principal editor of *Crossing Centuries: The New Generation in Russian Poetry,* he is known for his translations of Nina Iskrenko, Ivan Zhdanov, and Alexei Parschikov, among others. A former Fulbright professor at Moscow State Linguistics University, he currently teaches in the MFA creative writing program at LIU Brooklyn.